KU-772-374

Bamberg
for Newcomers and old Friends

A Guide to the Town by Karin Dengler-Schreiber

Translation by Rosemary Neberle

"Apple Woman", door knob in Eisgrube

See page 75 for opening times of museums,
cathedral etc.

Pictures:
Town map by Braun and Hogenberg 1617, based on engraving
by Petrus Zweidler (State Library Bamberg V B 23aa).
Star Mantle (Diocesan Museum Bamberg).
St. Kunigunde (Reinhold Eckert).
Farewell to the Apostles with view of town of Bamberg in 1483
(History Museum Bamberg).
Imperial tomb (Peter Eberts)
All other photos by Alfred Weinkauf

Second print 1996
© 1990, Bayerische Verlagsanstalt GmbH, Bamberg
All rights retained regarding reproduction and distribution,
including film, radio and television as well as
photocopying and printing of extracts.
Cover: Klaus Borowietz
Overall production: SOV Graphische Betriebe, Bamberg
Printed in Germany
ISBN 3-87052-271-2

History of the Town

Tour of the Town

Information in Brief

Index

Map of Town

Gemini sign of the zodiac on Emperor Henry II's Star Mantle, a gift to the emperor from the Apulian prince Melos on the occasion of his visit to Bamberg in 1019. A unique witness to the beginning of Bamberg's history, it is displayed in the Diocesan Museum.

History of the Town

The magic of history – in not many places can one experience it as intensely as in Bamberg. The walls are soaked with history and stories. Let us make some of them tell their tale. You must know the background history to understand the various works of art and perhaps experience what makes up the being and charm of this town. If you wander through the streets and alleyways on foot, you can, besides the important works of art, photographed innumerable times, make many small discoveries: the figure of a camel on a house and rusty Baroque door hinges, little heads as fasteners for shutters and the Rider from the cathedral in a tattooer's shop, carved banisters and garden gnomes in a monastery garden. This little book is intended as a thread for sleuths to follow.

Beginnings

History goes back a long way in Bamberg. Latest excavations on the cathedral hill showed that there was a large fortress there as early as the 7th century, in which Slavs and Franks lived together peacefully. It was situated on one of the foothills of the Steiger Forest, fairly high above the Regnitz, and guarded the river crossing and two important roads: one, stretching in a north-south direction through the Carolingian Empire from Lübeck to Regensburg, ran east of the right arm of the Regnitz; the other over St. James's Hill came from Würzburg in the west and continued in the direction of Forchheim.

The fortress was in the hands of the Babenbergers, after whom the later town was named, in the 9th century. After the tragic end of the family, the for-

7th cent. Slavonic and Frankish fortress

9th cent. Babenbergers

tress passed into the hands of the German king. Emperor Otto II gave the *civitas papinberc* to his cousin, the Bavarian duke Henry the Quarrelsome, in 973. It is said of his son, the later Emperor Henry II (1002–1024), that he loved the place deeply even as a child. When he married Kunigunde of Luxembourg in 997, he gave her Bamberg as her "morning gift" (gift given to a bride by her husband after the wedding night).

Henry's "morning gift" to Kunigunde

Capital of the Empire

Foundation of the bishopric

After Henry had been elected German king in 1002, he decided to found a bishopric here. Apart from his personal preferences, religious and above all political motives were the decisive factors. At that time bishops were the king's most important civil servants and were also appointed by him. Bamberg lay between the two blocks of power, the dukedom of Saxony and the dukedom of Bavaria, and near the eastern border of the empire. It was therefore necessary for the king to have a reliable man at his bidding there. The first Bamberg bishop, Eberhard (1007–1040), was at the same time chancellor of the empire, that is to say its highest administrative official. Henry's considerations were fulfilled in the long term: loyalty to the empire was a constant factor in Bamberg politics.

The first bishop

Emperor Henry II had a second, very much more far-reaching plan. The fact that he furnished the bishopric and the cathedral he had built in an imperial manner and other signs lead one to the conclusion that he intended erecting the symbolic capital of the empire in Bamberg, on "seven hills" and with a church of St. Peter like the ancient imperial city of Rome. Abbot Gerhard of Seeon called Bamberg *caput orbis,* capital of the world. Emperor Henry II and his consort Kunigunde held court in Bamberg very often and endowed the place with all sorts of possessions: including six royal abbeys and scattered property in South Germany, in Alsace and Carinthia. Bamberg owes them thanks for even more though: priceless books, including those of the bibliophile

The "new Rome"

6

emperor Otto III, holy relics, works of art and their state robes; but material for legends, too. The recording of the latter formed the basis for the canonization of Henry (1146) and Kunigunde (1200). Even today they are both almost omnipresent in the town – on altars and bridges, the fronts of houses and in narrative.

Canonization of Henry and Kunigunde

What an outstanding position Bamberg held is proved by the fact that the summit meeting of the two great powers of that time took place here: at Easter 1020, Pope Benedict VIII visited Emperor Henry II in Bamberg to discuss the fate of the empire and the papal states with him and also to consecrate some churches on this occasion.

Pope's visit in 1020

Pope Clement II, effigy from his tomb in the cathedral (after 1225)

City of Bishops

Pope Clement II

The second Bamberg bishop, Suidger (1040–1047), was elected pope, as Clement II, at the behest of Henry III. "I will take every care to protect Thee, Bamberg, my friend, my sister, my bride, my dove", wrote Clement II shortly before his death, which suddenly overtook the relatively young man only nine months after his election. It was his express wish to be buried in Bamberg. Under dramatic circumstances his body was transported secretly to Bamberg. His tomb is in the west chancel of the cathedral, the only papal tomb north of the Alps.

Cathedral school: the school of the empire

Emperor Henry II's successors forgot the idea of a capital. Bamberg grew into a new role: of being *the* school of the empire. Anyone who wanted to make a career for himself in Germany had to have gone through the Bamberg cathedral school. They had a command of not only classical and Christian literature; Bishop Gunther (1057–1065) even amused himself with German epic poetry to the dismay of many a cathedral canon.

At his wish the scholar Ezzo wrote a song in German that, in an intellectual world dominated by Latin, marks the "new beginning for vernacular literature". The Bamberg canons were very proud of their education; they rejected a business-minded but rather uneducated bishop, Hermann I, so vehemently that, in the end, he had to resign.

Bischop Otto I

In comparison, Bishop Otto I (1102–1139) was immensely popular. In 1189 the Bambergers achieved his canonization. He was an exceptional genius in matters of organization and finance and a remarkably likeable person. In a period of great military conflict, he managed not to take part in a single war and played a decisive part in ending the pernicious quarrel between the emperor and pope about the appointment (investiture) of the bishops. He became best known as *Apostolus Pomeranorum* because of his two missionary journeys to the Pomeranians. He founded and reformed numerous monasteries and was the builder of many churches, in Bamberg, too.

There, in the course of the 11th century, the

Benedictine monastery of St. Michael (1015) and the collegiate churches of St. Stephen (1020), St. James (1072) and St. Gangolf (1070) grew up round the cathedral like the points of a cross. Each of them lay in a rather large area protected by walls or hedges, where, together with the clerics, the "people" of the chapter or monastery lived, the servants and craftsmen and, especially on the Michelsberg hill, the wine-growers who produced the wine on its slopes. These so-called "immunities" were independent legal districts, in which the abbot or prior had powers to rule, comparable to a certain extent to those of a mayor and a judge. The "Immunities"

In the meanwhile, a traders' settlement had developed at the foot of the cathedral hill on the banks of the Regnitz, the core of the later bourgeois town. Sandstrasse formed its axis; the marketplace was situated there, the town court, the episcopal mint and the large courtyard of the "customs men", the tax collectors of the bishop. The bishop namely was not only the spiritual leader of the bishopric, but also the worldly lord of the "ecclesiastic principality of Bamberg", of a small "state" with far-reaching territories. The bishop was furnished with all sovereign rights, such as his own mint, taxes and jurisdiction. The Beginnings of the bourgeois town The bishop as sovereign

The "Sand", the first bourgeois settlement at the foot of the cathedral hill

9

bishop remained prince of the ecclesiastic state and ruler over the town of Bamberg right up until secularization in 1802.

The Bourgeois Town

The bourgeois settlement in the Sand district had become too cramped for space at the beginning of the 12th century and it had spread across to the area of the island between the two arms of the Regnitz. The two parts of the town were linked by a bridge (the "Upper Bridge"), on which the townspeople built their town hall. Some large and rich patrician families **Patrician families** had grown up among them, who more and more took control of the fortunes of the "burgh" in the course of the 13th and 14th century. Soon after 1200 the citi- **Town seal** zens were granted a town seal. It shows the "knight" St. George with the eagle coat of arms of the Andechs-Meranier. The mightiest noble house in Upper Franconia in the period around 1200, they occupied the Bamberg bishop's throne almost without a break between 1177 and 1245. The rights of the town community developed during their era. From 1306 on the town charter came into being and it also attested the existence of a town council.

The citizens now wanted to play a part in intellectual and cultural life. The headmaster of the St. Gangolf school, Hugo von Trimberg, wrote a "best **Hugo von Trimberg** seller" around 1300, the lengthy moralizing poem called *"The Runner"*. He proffers the opinion that only he who can compose poetry in Latin and *German,* as well as read and write both, is a real man. Behind the claim for an equal footing for German lies a demand, that cannot be overhead, for education for the citizens and the opening of the ecclesiastical-noble schools.

The rich patrician families invested their capital in something quite innovative for that time: the special **Market-gardens** cultivation of vegetables, market-gardens that they set up on land cleared in Hauptsmoor Forest east of the right arm of the Regnitz. They thereby added the **Bamberg's three components** third component of the structure of Bamberg as is still valid today: it grew together out of the spiritual

10

St. Kunigunde on the Lower Bridge

town on the hills, the bourgeois trading town on the island and the agricultural market-gardening town.

The growing power of the citizens was a thorn in the flesh of the cathedral chapter – 20 canons, who stood by the bishop's side in spiritual and secular matters, but who increasingly outvoted him. The cathedral chapter also had the say in the immunities, whose inhabitants, in contrast to the citizens in the "burgh", did not have to pay any taxes, were not subject to the municipal court, did not contribute to the upkeep of bridges, roads and towers and whose markets were exempt from tax. These conditions were naturally highly unfavourable to the townspeople. In addition the cathedral chapter prevented the **Town wall** building of a town wall, for such a large, communal task had always resulted in a strengthening of the self-confidence and unity of communities. In 1430, **Hussites** the only way to stop the Hussites from looting and burning the inadequately fortified town was to pay the immense sum of 15,000 guilders as ransom. In **"Taxpayers'** 1435 the "Taxpayers' War" broke out, a conflict be-**War"** tween the bishop and cathedral chapter on the one side and the citizens on the other, which the townspeople lost. Many of the great families left Bamberg and took their capital with them. The town did not recover from this blood-letting for a long time. In the high Middle Ages Bamberg had all that was needed to develop into a city, after 1435 it remained no more than the seat of the bishop and capital of the Bamberg ecclesiastic principality.

The Good Times in the late Middle Ages

In the late Middle Ages the scales of power were **Cathedral** tipped more and more clearly in favour of the cathe-**chapter** dral chapter. The bishop moved from the cathedral **and bishop** hill to Altenburg Castle. From the 14th century on the castle was converted into expensively furnished apartments for the bishop. Intellectual open-mindedness and an appreciation of art were a mark of the Bamberg episcopal court in the late Middle Ages.

12

The "Wise Virgins" on the Wedding Porch of the Upper Parish Church (1350)

Bishops, nobility and the rich patrician class supported and paid large numbers of artists, sometimes for reasons of competitive showing-off. In addition to the smaller craftmen's workshops, larger firms grew up with a large number of journeymen who could afford to study developments in European art. The Bamberg artists grasped the innovations coming from Italy and the Netherlands quicker than elsewhere in the first half of the 15th century. 9 painters and wood-carvers were at work in Bamberg around 1500, including Wolfgang Katzheimer, Ulrich Widmann, Paul Lautensack, Conrad Busser and Hans Nussbaum. But Hans Pleydenwurff, the most talented of a Bamberg family of painters, had already migrated to Nuremberg in the wake of Bamberg patrician money and enticed by the privileges the imperial city offered. This development caused the Bamberg art market to dry up after 1520.

Today not much is left in Bamberg of the rich production of and up to the late Middle Ages. The

Art in its prime

Painters and wood-carvers

devastation carried out by Margrave Albrecht Alcibiades and the Thirty Years' War, the change to Baroque and secularization either destroyed the works of art or dispersed them.

It is however not art alone that testifies to Bamberg's flourishing intellectual life in the 15th century. Bamberg became one of the centres of German humanism, of the arts and natural sciences under the bishops Georg I von Schaumberg (1459–1475) and Georg III, Schenk von Limpurg (1505–1522). Johann von Schwarzenberg (1463–1528), the author of the *"Bamberg Penal Code"*, was one of the important men at the court of Georg III. The Bamberg bishop's court was also interested in new inventions. It is no mere chance therefore that the new art of printing was practised in Bamberg, the second town to do so after Mainz. The first-ever illustrated printed book was conceived in Bamberg in 1460/61. The cathedral canon, Albrecht von Eyb (1420–75), wrote not only a poem about the town's beauty, but also one about the beauty of a girl called Barbara. In his *"Appellatio"* the Bamberg women call for the introduction of free love. No wonder that he expressed the opinion: "If Nuremberg were mine, I would want to consume it in Bamberg!"

Apparently one could lead a good life here in those days. Many written works extol the town as a fertile garden; the Bamberg gardeners' skills in improving the growing of fruit and vegetables had success and did much to refine gastronomic culture. Beer consumption per person is said to have been 440 litres annually in 1450.

The architectural structure of the town also took on firm contours at the time. The old cores of the various settlements grew together. A large number of houses in the Old Town still date from the Middle Ages, even if outwardly refashioned in Baroque style, as do the shape and size of the building plots, the course of the streets and the lay-out of many a square. Even today one would find one's way, with few exceptions, in the centre of the town by using Petrus Zweidler's map of 1602 (see page 2, inside cover).

Humanism

The art of printing

Beer consumption

Petrus Zweidler

14

Troubled Times in the 16th and 17th Century

There were a lot of supporters of the Reformation Reformation in Bamberg during the rule of Bishop Georg III, Schenk von Limpurg. Many of them had to leave the town though in the time of his successor, Weigand von Redwitz. What angered people most was the banishing of one of the canons of St. Gangolf, Johannes Schwanhausen, whose sermons on the unjust distribution of wordly goods had attracted a large number of listeners. So all sorts of motives – social reform, reformist, emotional and the renewed attempt of the citizens to break the power of the cathedral chapter led to the Bamberg Revolt, as part Bamberg Revolt during Peasants' Revolt of the great German revolution that we call the Peasants' Revolt, on 11th April 1525. The townspeople occupied the town gates, the outraged mob looted the residences of the cathedral canons, who had fled, and Michaelsberg Monastery. Then a peaceful settlement with Bishop Weigand was brought about. Yet after the defeat of the peasants' army before the gates of Würzburg, not even his pleas could stop the punitive expedition led by the "peasant butcher", Georg von Truchsess. The cathedral chapter had called in the troops behind Weigand's back. 12 rebels were executed in Bamberg and town and country were disciplined with extremely high compensation fines.

A country generally pays a high price for failing to carry out reforms. Revenge for the 1525 revolution, which had been thrashed to death, came 100 years later. The horrific 30 Years' War began in 1618 and The 30 Years' War reached Franconia in 1631. The troops often passed through the territory of the Bamberg principality and so it was particularly affected, was looted and devastated by both friend and enemy, imperial forces, the Swedes and the French equally. There were areas which, by the end of the war, had been up to 80% depeopled, the people shot, tortured to death, they died of starvation and epidemics. Defence of Bamberg was not possible with its many separate districts and its weak walls and it was taken again and again. Before the war the town had about 12,000 inhabitants, after it barely 7,000. In 1643 the government had "the abandoned and desolate houses" recorded. Of the 660 dwellings affected, 25% stood empty, 25% were in fact lived in but in dire need of repair, 50% however were "in total ruin".

Even before this, Bamberg had much to suffer. **Witch-hunts** From 1628 onwards, the witch-hunts, instigated by those in authority, raged with even greater intensification. In the principality of Bamberg hundreds of people, above all women but also men and children, were their victims, undergoing unimaginable tortures. Bishop Fuchs von Dornheim played a particularly prominent role, even also confiscating 500,000 guilders from those executed. The Middle Ages were not dark, the 17th century certainly was.

Madonna on corner of a house, No. 3 Frauenstrasse

16

The Schönborn Age

The devastated land recovered slowly. A kind of economic miracle broke out under the rule of the Schönborn bishops – Lothar Franz (1693–1729) and Friedrich Karl (1729–1746). To begin with, this necessitated the reforms Prince Bishop Lothar Franz carried through in administration and economy. A prince reigning with absolute power, he created a firmly organized, well-functioning staff of bourgeois civil servants. The state now controlled every area of life and took on many new obligations. Regulations were imposed on commerce and the trades, manufacturing was promoted, roads built and an attempt was made to get the upper hand of poverty. The measures carried out by the Counter-Reformation stabilized the Catholic Church and were an additional help.

Schönborn bishops

Bourgeois civil servants

Counter-Reformation

Madonna, No. 6 Zinkenwörth

The colourfulness of the Middle Ages with its gaudy colours and deep shadows gradually made way for the well-ordered and clearly illuminated bureaucratic state.

The most important matter now was to show who one was. The significance and purpose of mighty buildings was to show off one's own, perhaps only imagined, importance. The sudden explosion of an obsession with building in the "Schönborn Age" can only be explained by this fact. Bamberg must have been one enormous building site in the 18th century. Numerous monumental buildings were erected – first of all the prince bishop's New Residence, in addition churches, monasteries and palaces. Tax benefits **Change to Baroque** enabled the townpeople as well to give their houses a new face with Baroque façades. Fountains, bridges and squares were adorned with statues. Behind all

16.-century half-timbered house with Baroque façade, No. 24 Kapuziner-strasse

this was the architectural conception of the sovereign, the bishop. Of course a mediaeval town like Bamberg, which had grown naturally and was made up of so many small details, did not allow an ideal symmetrical plan to be imposed on it. The town planning of the prince bishops, following Balthasar Neumann's ideas, intended a Baroque axis from the east side of the town, from the famous bridge called Seesbrücke (destroyed 1784, Kettenbrücke the present replacement) along Hauptwachstrasse, then Grüner Markt street, through the archway of the island town hall and right up to the cathedral square. Along the axis buildings were constructed which served as architectural models for other bourgeois buildings. They tried to create visual links between them and an impression of space, in accordance with the Baroque feeling for life. The climax comes with the corner pavilion of the New Residence, which visually links the hilly part of the town, the island part and the surrounding countryside.

Balthasar Neumann

New Residence

Social Reforms and Secularization

Other problems came to the fore towards the end of the 18th century; the social situation became more and more depressing. Franz Ludwig von Erthal, Prince Bishop of Bamberg and Würzburg (1779–1795), tried to remedy the deplorable state of affairs with far-reaching reforms in the legal system, education, health and care of the poor. He was the prototype of the "enlightened" prince, who saw himself as the servant of his people. With the greatest possible thrift, he used all the monies at his disposal to improve the conditions of his subjects. There were about 21,000 inhabitants in Bamberg at that time, 212 of them members of religious orders and 162 secular priests, 1,624 master craftsmen, 1,003 journeymen and 208 apprentices, in addition 1,400 in service and 3,000 registered poor. Together with his personal physician, Adalbert Friedrich Marcus, Franz Ludwig had the then most modern hospital in Europe built in 1789. At the same time he created a kind of "health insurance" for those in service and journeymen, to which employers and employees had

Franz Ludwig von Erthal (1779–1795)

Hospital care

19

to make contributions. The organization of the primary school system was to enable his subjects to improve their situation by their own efforts. His system for the care of the poor was considered so exemplary that the kingdom of Bavaria adopted it in 1816 and its essential features retained their validity until the introduction of Bismarck's social measures.

School system

Care of the poor

However, individuals like him could no longer prevent the revolution of Europe. In the wake of the Napoleonic Wars secularization had been decided on in 1801: the German princes were to be compensated with secularized ecclesiastical regions to the right of the Rhine to make up for their losses to the left of the river. "We shall hand over the piece of material from which they will cut to shape compensations for both friend and enemy", Prince Bishop Franz Ludwig had prophesied. Bavarian troops occupied the town in 1802; thus the independent ecclesiastic principality of Bamberg came to an end, since then Bamberg has belonged to Bavaria.

Secularization

Annexation by Bavaria

Bourgeois Emancipation and Years of Expansion

The former royal seat was just one provincial town among many in the strictly centralistically organized Bavaria. Not even the small court of a branch of the Wittelsbachers, who were allocated the "New Residence", could make any difference. The university was closed, the seat of the military government was transferred to Bayreuth. Bamberg retained the appeal court (now the Upper Regional Court), state library and state archives. In 1817 it was raised to the status of archbishopric for North Bavaria.

Archbishopric for North Bavaria

Cultural life up to that time had been sustained by the bishop's court, the cathedral chapter and the monasteries. With their dissolution the bourgeoisie took over this role and, now that they were freed from traditional constraints, developed enormous activity. Over 100 cultural and social societies were formed. Their collections and 30 private collectors absorbed cultural possessions that had been dumped during secularization – altars, paintings, gold and silver chalices and crosses, manuscripts and books, furniture and many other things. Citizens' initiatives saved Altenburg Castle, St. James's Church (Jakobskirche) and St. Sebastian's Chapel from being pulled down. As early as 1802 Count Soden had founded a permanent theatre that, continuously tottering on the brink of ruin, could be kept going only with difficulty. E.T.A. Hoffmann was engaged as director of music at the theatre in 1808. He gathered plenty of material for his literary production in Bamberg, that was considered a prototype of the "romantic town", but he did not feel very happy here. "Now I've served my years of apprenticeship and martyrdom in Bamberg", he noted on the day of his departure in 1813.

Count Soden

E.T.A. Hoffmann

E.T.A. Hoffmann House, No. 26 Schillerplatz, where the poet lived from 1808–13

21

George F. W. Hegel The philosopher Georg F. W. Hegel edited a progressive newspaper here from 1807 till 1809, failed because of censorship, just as his successor did, the **F. Gottlob Wetzel** poet Friedrich Gottlob Wetzel. Politically Bambergers, the lawyer Nikolaus Titus in particular, belonged to the pioneers of the democratic movement and to the leading figures at the assembly in St. Paul's Church in Frankfurt. The failure of the movement after 1848, the arrest and expulsion of its leaders, caused every activity in this direction to wane.

New transport communications opened up the **Canal and railway** town. The old Danube-Main Canal with Bamberg as its northern end was finished in 1841. As early as 1844 there was the linking with the new rail network. **Beginning industrialization** From 1870 on industrialization also gained a foothold. The new factories were not very large, a lot of small and medium-sized firms formed, as today, a healthy basis in the economic life of the town. The Bambergers were to some extent very proud of their industry – pictures show the cathedral towers almost disappearing in a forest of factory chimneys. But they did not want to become a real industrial city; the social changes involved were too worrying. The population multiplied to about 50,000 by 1910. New roads and districts were laid out, the town grew, in particular to the south and east.

Idyllic garden scene in Little Venice

22

The Jews had an important share in the economic and cultural life of the town. After the laws limiting the number allowed to live in the town had been lifted in the middle of the 19th century, they moved in from the surrounding countryside. There were about 1,000 Jewish citizens in Bamberg in 1933. This large community had been completely extinguished by the end of the Third Reich, the synagogue was burnt down in the so-called "Crystal Night", almost all traces of the history of the Jews in Bamberg wiped out. It is only fairly recently that they have been remembered again.

The Jewish community

The Two World Wars and the Third Reich

Outwardly the First World War left no marks on the town, but Bamberg mourned the loss of 1,330 killed in action. After Kurt Eisner had proclaimed a republic in Munich on 8th November 1918, a 54-man workers', townspeople's and soldiers' council took control in Bamberg, although they allowed state and civic authorities to continue to exist. With an application to become seat of the National Assembly, they were consciously establishing a link with the tradition of 1848. However the preference was for Weimar (hence Weimar Republic). But the basic position of the inhabitants remained conservative, as the state parliament elections of January 1919 showed. This caused the Bavarian prime minister, Johannes Hoffmann, and his cabinet to seek refuge in Bamberg from the unrest in Munich after the murder of Kurt Eisner on 7th April 1919. Here they prepared the constitution that was adopted on 14th August 1919 and remained in force until 1933.

Republic

Constitution of 1919

The Bavarian People's Party generally emerged from the elections in the following years as the strongest political force. It was supported by a fundamental consensus of the citizens, a feeling of obligation to tradition and the Catholic Church, which expressed itself in the impressive celebration of the 900th anniversary of Emperor Henry's death in 1924. In the elections for the Reichstag on 24th April 1932, however, the National Socialists became the strongest party for the first time. After the takeover of power in 1933, the so-called "Gleichschaltung", that is forcing into line, was carried out with speed and brutality in Bamberg. Those who opposed or criticized it, like the former lord mayor Weegmann, were taken into preventive detention. The growing opposition of the Catholic Church in fact made Bamberg a town "not to be relied on" in Hitler's eyes, but could no longer hinder the course of events. The Jewish population of Bamberg was driven out or murdered, as were others who put up resistance to National Socialism. There is a memorial plaque to them on the Old Town Hall on the Lower Bridge, alongside a plaque in memory of the 3,700 killed in action or missing in the Second World War. The air raids on Bamberg in 1945 cost 378 people their lives, 6,800 became homeless. It is only in comparison with the terrible devastation that other towns had to suffer that one can say Bamberg got off rather lightly.

Takeover of power 1933

Forcing into line by National Socialism

Damage in the Second World War

World Heritage and Regional Centre

The basic structure of the town and its most important edifices remained untouched though. The changes in the years following 1945 did more to destroy the architecture in German towns and villages than the war. In Bamberg, the process however was very restrained and this factor played a decisive role in the appearance of the town today. In 1981 the Old Town with its almost 1,400 listed buildings was declared a town monument as a whole. There is a widespread awareness that the intrinsic value of this old town is irreplaceable. More than in any other German community, the Bambergers invest in the preservation of their old buildings. The university has several chairs in the field of conservation of ancient monuments, citizens' action groups fight for the preservation of architectural heritage in a manner both committed and sometimes even irksome. All these factors taken together led to Bamberg being put on the "World Heritage List" by UNESCO on 11. 12. 1993, for the reason that Bamberg represents "the

Town as a monument

Restoration and redevelopment measures

central European city as developed from an early-mediaeval basic structure in a most unique way".

Yet, under the historic mantle, Bamberg is a town very much alive and of central importance for a wide area. It is an administrative centre with about 30 regional offices and an educational centre with a wealth of technical and special schools, 27 primary schools, 3 secondary modern, 11 grammar schools and a university (8,000 students). It has its own theatre, 25 orchestras, including the world-famous "Bamberg Symphony", and a remarkable range of libraries, archives and museums to offer. The "Klinikum" (polyclinic) was finished in 1984, the "Concert and Congress Hall" at the far end of the "Weide" square in 1993, both providing facilities for a large catchment area.

Administration

Schools

Cultural life

An economic factor with a continuous rate of growth is tourism. There were 255,000 overnight stays in 1994, although numerous visitors only stop to enjoy the "dream city" while just passing through. Bamberg's economic basis lies hidden behind the "dream city" image and is not visible at a first glance.

Tourism

Economy

A landscape of roofs and towers: St. Stephen's, Upper Parish Church, Carmelite Church, Altenburg Castle, cathedral

25

Three large and over 70 medium-sized firms with about 15,000 employed in industry and over 35,000 commuters also make Bamberg the economic centre of Upper Franconia. There is a wide variety of manufactured goods: textiles and leather goods, engineering and electro-technical factories among others.

From these few details one can foresee what the greatest present and future problem for the town will be: dealing with the traffic. 46,000 cars licenced in Bamberg are a hopeless overtaxing of the historical streets. The opening of the "Iron Curtain" in autumn 1989 has shifted Bamberg from its border situation back to a position in the middle. Its role as a communications junction only increases the difficulties. A lot of imagination and courage will be needed to get the upper hand of them.

Traffic situation

The hope is not unfounded that Bamberg will find a way out of the past, and yet with it, into the future. It is still an architectural jewel with an open heart – a place to live in, to get to know, of human proportions. It is a lovable gem with scratches and wrinkles, where the splendid works of art are set in worn steps, sagging roof ridges and brightly polished door handles – all those little things that do our souls so much good in these times of materialized rationality.

Baroque mask on house, No. 2 Pfahlplätzchen

Tour of the Town

The Town on the Hills

The *cathedral square* was the germ cell of Bamberg. The fortress of the Babenbergers stood there. Emperor Henry II erected his palace and his cathedral there, the seat of the government was there and the spiritual and wordly centre of the ecclesiastic principality of Bamberg. Today it harmoniously unites the most important styles of architecture in German art history: high Romanesque, early Gothic, Renaissance, Baroque and Rococo round a large majestic space, which is one of the most beautiful squares in Germany.

Cathedral square

The *cathedral* of St. Peter and St. George stands on the site of the cathedral built by Henry II, which was consecrated in the presence of all the bishops of the empire in 1012. It was extremely richly appointed, as recent excavations have proved. The church burnt down the night before Easter 1081. It was soon rebuilt; Bishop Otto the Holy (1102–1139) in particular did much to beautify the cathedral. But in summer 1185 another devastating fire struck the church and indeed all the surrounding buildings. Bishop Ekbert von Andechs-Meranien (1203–1237) had a new cathedral built after his return from exile from about 1215 onwards. Thanks to his wealth and his good connections all over Europe, he was able to afford the best architects and stonemasons' guilds then on the market. Stylistically one can identify four different masons' guilds. They built a pillared basilica with two chancels built over crypts, a transept at the west end and 4 towers. Their work was not yet finished when the cathedral was consecrated on 6th May 1237.

Cathedral

History of building

27

The tempestuous development in the art of that period – the transition from Romanesque to Gothic – can be clearly read, a fascinating experience, from the architecture and sculptures of the cathedral. Some of the forms seen though were not dictated by the period but consciously chosen for their symbolic message. To name one example, a ground plan with two chancels was chosen, something completely old-fashioned for the early 13th century, but intended to recall the cathedral of Henry II, who had been made a saint in the meantime (1146).

The cathedral, consecrated in 1237. View of the east chancel

28

The building was begun with the richly decorated east apse, which faces the valley and the town. The everyday entrances to the cathedral are in the two east towers. *Adam's Portal,* the oldest cathedral por- tal, leads into the south aisle. It has a rounded arch adorned with a zigzag frieze. The six figures that used to stand under the canopies are now installed in the Diocesan Museum. The portal was the main entrance for pilgrims coming to the tomb of the founder of the bishopric. Statues of the saints, Henry and Kuni-gunde, greeted the visitor. Henry's left foot is some-what raised, resting on a stone, the basis for a legend that tells of a hunting injury of the emperor. He turns towards his wife, who is wearing unusual apparel, different from the other female figures in the cathe-dral. Kunigunde was canonized in 1200. On account of the virginity which was ascribed to her, she was put on a status close to the Mother of God, who was worshipped most fervently at that time. Worship of Kunigunde gradually began to outshine that of Henry. That is why she was placed in the middle of the left reveal, as the most important figure. She is handing St. Stephen standing next to her a model of a church, to symbolize her founding of St. Stephen's Church. On the right reveal once stood the cathedral patron saint Peter together with Adam and Eve, the first life-size nude figures in mediaeval art.

The *Lady Portal* in the northeast tower displays the Madonna in the tympanum, enthroned between the cathedral's patron saints, Peter and George, and the founders, Henry and Kunigunde. The small fig-ures in the spandrels and at the feet of the Madonna could be members of the Andechs-Meranier House: the builder of the cathedral, Bishop Ekbert, his uncle, the cathedral dean Poppo, and the (kneeling) crusader, Count Otto, who was punished as an acces-sory, when the German king, Philip of Swabia, was murdered in Bamberg in 1208. The sculptures on the Lady Portal are the oldest belonging to the cathedral and were created by members of the so-called "older workshop" around 1217. The Romanesque metal buttons to the right of the portal illustrate the meas-urements of the cathedral: a cubit of 67 cm. and a foot of 26.8 cm. in length (5:2 ratio).

Cathedral Main entrance to the cathedral for the solemn
Princes' Portal procession of the prince bishop was the *Princes'
Portal* (1224/25). On the funnel shape of the reveals,
the Apostles are standing on the shoulders of the
Prophets, a symbol of the link between Old and New
Testament. They have been damaged by wind ero-
sion; the experts are still debating over the best measures to protect them. The tympanum with a depiction
of the Last Judgment is dominated by Christ as judge
of the world. Mary and John at his feet are pleading
for the small figures arising from their coffins. The
blessed push forward behind Mary, their joy is
reflected in the faces of the three smaller figures on
the extreme left. A king is among the blessed; angels
are bringing the tools of torment. The damned on the
right are being dragged down into the abyss with a
chain held by a devil grinning with malicious joy.
Neither power nor riches can help them: king, bishop
and pope and even the rich man with his sack of
money are lost. The screaming desperation in their
faces and the glowing joy of the blessed belong to the
earliest and most expressive portrayals of feelings in
European art. But it is not this innovation alone that
makes the sculptures on Princes' Portal so unusual
and revolutionary for their time. Details, too, are
further evidence: Christ robed to the neck shows the
wound in His side and thus the transition from the
Romanesque Christ as King to the Gothic Christ
Suffering; an everyday gesture, like the wicked ges-
ticulation of the damned king in the direction of the
Devil, had never before been so depicted in art;
hierarchical proportions have also been thrown out –
the Devil is larger than Mary and John. The Princes'
Portal, especially if compared with the serene order
of the Lady Portal, makes the whole suspense of its
period of conception, a time when the old rules were
broken, "sculpturally" visible.

St. Vitus's *St. Vitus's Portal,* with a delicate rosette above it
Portal made by the Ebrach stonemasons, opens into the
West transept. The west towers, modelled on Laon cathe-
towers dral, had a middle spire surrounded by four small
turrets until 1766.

Princes' Portal, main entrance to the cathedral, 1224/25, "Last Judgment" in the tympanum

Tour of the Cathedral

The interior of the cathedral expresses a feeling of suspense between the serenity of late-Romanesque in *St. George's Choir* and the heavenwards soaring of the early Gothic in *St. Peter's Choir* at the west end. The putative uniformity is highly astonishing in view of the fact that the plans were altered almost every winter during the good 20 years of building. One of the decisive questions involved was whether the cathedral should have a flat wooden ceiling like St. Henry's cathedral or a modern and firepoof vault. Since restoration in 1973, the cleansed walls and

St. George's Choir

St. Peter's Choir

pillars have regained the clear colours of the Franconian sandstone. But the church has only had this
appearance since the "purification of style" ordered by King Ludwig I of Bavaria, which removed all the postmediaeval furnishings of the cathedral between 1828 and 1837.

At the time of its construction in the first half of the 13th century the building was painted in bright
colours. Traces can still be seen on the *reliefs of the choir parcloses.* The lively discussions being held by the Apostles and the Prophets recall the mood of intellectual change which had seized the whole of Europe and led, among other things, to the founding of the first universities. There the dialectic method superseded the strict belief in the old authorities. Some of the peculiarities of the figures of the Apostles on the south choir parcloses are derived from examples of plastic art in painting: folds that fall upwards, pillarlike legs, feet spread out at an angle. The transition to three-dimensionality was only completed with the Prophets in the north aisle. One can believe it is possible to read the joy of the sculptors that the figures detached themselves from the surface behind them and were now really mobile – to be seen in the extreme turns of the body that are depicted.

The figure of *Pope Clement II* (d. 1047) stands on the left pillar in the north aisle. The tomb of the former Bamberg bishop in the west chancel, the only papal tomb north of the Alps, is not accessible. The figure used to lie on the slab of the tomb. Traces of the original painting are quite clearly visible. The
seeress *(Elizabeth)* opposite him and *Mary* are generally described as a Visitation group. This interpretation, which would depict the moment when Elizabeth meets Mary and realizes that she is carrying the Saviour, is not very likely, since the two figures, even if they stood opposite each other, would look past one another. The *Laughing Angel* looks pleased that
he may give the martyr's crown to *St. Denis,* who is carrying his head in his arm. Nowadays we no longer know where these figures stood originally, nor to which sculptural programme they belonged and who
created them. The art historians differentiate between an "older" and "younger" workshop (the

32

The "Bamberg Rider" (after 1225), perhaps a portrayal of King Stephen of Hungary

Lady Portal, for example, dates from the older one, the Synagogue figure from the younger: the transition took place on the Princes' Portal about 1225), but the names of the sculptors have not been handed down. So many things about the erection of this church are not known and mysterious and we have only few contemporary reports.

Notwithstanding the work carried out by many scholars, the greatest mystery remains the most famous sculpture in the cathedral: the *Bamberg Rider*. Even to this day we do not know who this handsome young king is supposed to portray: Emperor Henry II, Emperor Constantine the Great or one of the Three Magi. Other interpretations

Cathedral

Bamberg Rider

favoured the Hohenstaufen king Konrad III (d. in Bamberg 1152, buried in the cathedral), King Philip of Swabia (murdered in Bamberg 1208) or Emperor Friedrich II (1212–1250). In any case the Rider is considered to represent the "ideal of a king and knight at the height of the Middle Ages", an ideal used shamelessly by Nazi propaganda for its own purposes. It seems to me that a whole set of clues speak for St. Stephen, King of Hungary. He was Emperor Henry II's brother-in-law and the builder of the cathedral, Bishop Ekbert von Andechs-Meranien, also had very links with Stephen's successors through his sister, who was married to the Hungarian king.

Ecclesia and Synagogue   The figures of *Ecclesia* and *Synagogue* stand before the south choir parcloses. They used to flank the Princes' Portal and were, like the *Angel sounding the Last Trumpet* and *Abraham with the Souls of the Just*

The seeress, Elizabeth (after 1225)

34

next to them, saved from further weathering by installing them here in 1936. Ecclesia is the embodiment of the Church and her crown designates her as the sovereign. *Synagogue* is portrayed as the defeated, blindfolded and her staff broken; the tablets with the Ten Commandments seem to be just slipping from the grasp of her beautifully carved left hand. Together with Elizabeth, she is surely the most moving of the famous Bamberg sculptures from the first half of the 13th century described so far.

Between the two flights of steps leading up to the east choir stands the *Imperial Tomb.* The Würzburg sculptor, Tilman Riemenschneider, and his men worked on the tomb, which is made of Jura marble, from 1499 to 1513. On the slab the recumbent effigies of the imperial couple, Henry and Kunigunde, rest under canopies. The reliefs on the sides of the tomb depict the legends which have grown up round the

Synagogue, personification of Judaism (after 1225)

two saints: Kunigunde's ordeal by fire, when the empress had to walk barefoot over red-hot ploughshares to prove her innocence; the miracle of the penny during the building of St. Stephen's, when the workers could not take more than their "fair wage" from the bowl Kunigunde held out to them; the emperor's death; the weighing-up of his soul by the Archangel Michael and St. Benedict curing Henry of a stone complaint that had attacked him in Monte Cassino. The figures are wearing the dress in fashion in the period around 1500; the pilgrims could identify themselves immediately with them and recognize problems of their own world in the scenes portrayed – unjust accusation, the question of a "fair wage", illness, death and the fear of damnation – portrayed in a more elevated form but still a source of comfort.

Lady Altar by Veit Stoss
The south transept houses the *Lady Altar.* The most mature work by the 75-year-old Veit Stoss and carried out single-handed, it shows Christ's Nativity in the centre, which is why it is also called the Christmas Altar. The wings depict the Flight into Egypt, the Worship of the Magi, Nativity of Mary and Presentation in the Temple. Andreas Stoss, prior of the Nuremberg Carmelite monastery, had ordered

Imperial Tomb by Tilman Riemenschneider, 1513

36

*Lady Altar by
Veit Stoss, 1523.
Central panel
showing Christ's
Nativity*

the altar from his father in 1520. Veit Stoss had fallen
out of favour with the town council and his son
wanted to give him the chance to create a great work
following his own conceptions. Veit Stoss finished
the work in 1523, which then came to Bamberg after
the Reformation in Nuremberg. Andreas Stoss had
also retreated to Bamberg. At some unknown time,
the altar was robbed of some of its parts, including
the predella, the crown and four wing panels, frag-
ments of which are shown in the Diocesan Museum.
It was never painted; the lime wood, originally a
honey-yellow, was later stained dark. For a long
time, the altar served as a Nativity scene in the Upper
Parish Church, where it stood until 1937. The composition of the middle panel is no longer exactly the
same as the original. Yet the alteration did nothing to
blur the gentle, sometimes sad, smile of the figures
surrounding Mary.

Further works of art in the cathedral

North aisle: Annunciation relief (13th century). Kirchgattendorf Altar (Mary, Catherine and Barbara, around 1520). Madonna and Child (around 1240). Henry's altar and Kunigunde's with the head relics of the saints (1937/1951). Monument to Bishop Friedrich v. Truhendingen (d. 1366). Monument to Bishop Albrecht v. Wertheim (d. 1421). Altar to Henry (a composition made up of various individual works of art, including Sebastian, Henry and Stephen). Mühlhausen Altar (Madonna with angels, end of 15th century).

Nave: main altar and ambo (by Klaus Backmund, 1974). St. Peter's Altar in the west choir (figures by Justus Glesker, 1648). Choir stalls (14th century).

South aisle: monument to Bishop Friedrich von Hohenlohe (d. 1352, one of the best works of art in the cathedral). Rosary painting in the sacrament chapel (around 1520).

The *cathedral cloisters* on the south side of the cathedral serve as a lapidarium, a collection of stone monuments. The *chapter house,* built 1730/33, is adjacent to the cloisters. It is a demonstration of the ability of the architect Balthasar Neumann, sensitive and yet individual, with respect for the high demands of the cathedral and yet of its own distinctive charac- ter. The *Diocesan Museum* is in the chapter house. The exhibits are a combination of the old cathedral treasure and the collection of the cathedral canon von Pölnitz, brought together in 1966. The fabrics displayed in the Stone Chamber are absolutely (ill. p. 4) unique in the world: *Emperor Henry's Star Mantle,* which was given to him by the South Italian prince Melos in 1020, the so-called *choir mantle of Kunigunde,* woven in Byzantium, the *shroud of Bishop Gunther* (d. 1065), that was presented to him in Byzantium on his way to Jerusalem because they believed he was the German king travelling incognito, and the *vestments of Pope Clement II* (d. 1047), which were removed from his tomb in 1942 and are Diocesan Museum the oldest, almost complete, set of papal vestments still existent. The figures belonging to Adam's Portal (1230/35) were brought into the museum to save them from further weathering (s. p. 29 above). The precious goldsmith works and works of art from Romanesque to Baroque, which are exhibited in further rooms, are a reflection of the power and standing of the bishopric of Bamberg.

The *Old Court* was once linked to the cathedral. The Old Court Henry II had his palace here and it became the bishop's palace, too, with the founding of the bishopric in 1007. Remains of the Romanesque building have been preserved and can be seen in the History Museum. The front of the building, facing the cathedral square, is determined by the *Chancery* Chancery Building *Building,* which Bishop Veit II had built by his architect, Asmus Braun, in the style of German Renaissance in 1568. The bishop's pride in his ances-

Inner courtyard of the Old Court

39

try is shown by the coats of arms on the Council Chamber's bay, the pride of the craftsman in his work by the figure of Braun at its foot. Originally the bay was painted.

The *"Beautiful Gate"* next to the Chancery building was created by the sculptor Pankraz Wagner in 1573. It is crowned by a relief showing Mary, flanked by Henry and Kunigunde with a model of the cathedral, St. Peter and St. George, on either side a personification of the rivers Main and Regnitz.

Through the gateway you enter the picturesque inner courtyard, encircled by half-timbered buildings. In summer it is the setting for the Calderon Festival open-air performances. The buildings with their high roofs were erected under the rule of the bishops Philipp von Henneberg, 1479 (coat of arms with the year over the west gate) and Heinrich III Gross von Trockau, 1487/89 (coat of arms carved by Adam Krafft over the gate to Karolinenstrasse).

At the moment the buildings are being restored to

provide an extension to the *History Museum,* which presents the history of the town and its surroundings from the Stone Age right up to 20th century painting. Its wealth of items cannot all be exhibited by any means. They mainly come from civic collections and endowments. Top items are the Romanesque *head of a knight,* the painting *"Farewell to the Apostles",* dated 1483, which shows the oldest existing view of the town of Bamberg, the large *wooden model* of the Church of the Fourteen Saints (Vierzehnheiligen) by Balthasar Neumann and sculptures by the Rococo sculptor Ferdinand Tietz. The museum is divided into different periods as well as into thematic groups (trade and crafts, faïence, armaments, astronomical instruments).

The third monumental building in the cathedral

square is the *New Residence.* Prince Bishop Johann Philipp von Gebsattel had the west part built by the Nuremberg city architect, Jakob Wolff the Elder, from 1605/11. The creator of the two wings facing the cathedral square was the Bamberg Prince Bishop and Elector of Mainz, Lothar Franz von Schönborn (1693–1729), "one of the most talented and impulsive princes ever to sit on the Bamberg bishop's throne".

On his election he was forced by the cathedral chapter into capitulation to an edict forbidding him "to build new palaces or to have old ones repaired at great expense". To begin with, this was an embarrassing fetter for his "building worm", as he called his passion for building. A general papal ban of such contracts freed him in 1697, a ban he had supported most energetically. He immediately gave his architect, Leonhard Dientzenhofer, orders to draw up plans for a "New Residence". As early as 1703, it was finished as it stands today. Further plans, by Balthasar Neumann among others, by which the Old Court would have been pulled down and replaced with a third wing of the Residence, could not be realized due to a lack of money (War of the Spanish Succession). The keystones jutting out on the corner

New Residence

**Leonhard
Dientzenhofer**

*New Residence,
built by Leonhard Dientzenhofer for
Prince Bishop
Lothar Franz
von Schönborn,
1703*

41

of the Residence by Obere Karolinenstrasse are the only surviving evidence of that project.

The wing of the Residence facing the town and ending with the soaring tower of the "Pavilion of the Fourteen Saints" is a demonstration of the Schönborn bishops' architectural ideals. At that time the whole of the cathedral square, which had been turned inwards like a mediaeval castle until then, was opened up to the town. The old gates fell, the level of the front of the square was dropped, an approach road made leading up from the town. From the surrounding countryside the wing of the Residence overlooking the town is a view visible from a great distance. The wing now houses the *State Library* with a splendid collection of old works, including 4,500 manuscripts dating from the 5th century on, 3,400 incunabula and 70,000 graphic prints.

The main portal in the south wing is accentuated by a gable decorated with figures above the pediment. A door to the left leads to the magnificently stuccoed stairwell of the Residence. That is where you can buy a ticket for the 45-minute guided tour of the *staterooms,* which are richly fitted with furniture, porcelain and tapestries. Their focal point is the *Emperor's Chamber* on the 2nd floor, a large room but not very high, which the court painter, Melchior Steidl, tried to give more height to by painting frescoes that lent an illusion of perspective between 1707 and 1709.

The *State Gallery,* on the 1st floor of the Gebsattel building, seems largely forgotten, although the Old German Gallery contains works of international standing, above all from the 15th and 16th century. The most interesting of these are *"Lucretia"* by Lucas Cranach the Elder and *"The Flood"* by Hans Baldung Grien. It also contains a few examples of the little-known Bamberg panel painting of the 15th century. The Baroque Gallery in the former courtiers' rooms in the same building unites works of top quality by German, Dutch and Flemish masters of the 17th and 18th century.

The wings of the Residence enclose the *Rose Garden.* Ferdinand Tietz's high-spirited statues with the scent of 1,000 rose bushes. Küchel's Rococo summer-

Façade of St. James's Church. Statue of St. James by Ferdinand Tietz

house (with café) and the view over the old roofs of the town and up to Michelsberg Monastery make the Rose Garden one of those summer experiences which are a must in Bamberg.

The *canonry courts,* many of them still mediaeval, built like little castles, still occupy the extensive site of the former cathedral fortress. They are all lived in and for that reason not usually open to the public. But it is worth wandering through the quiet alleyways behind the Old Court with their uneven cobbles, along the walls, over which jasmine and Virginia creeper hang down.

Canonry courts

The alleyways lead into the wide space of Obere Karolinenstrasse in front of the *Archbishop's Palace.* It was built by J. M. Küchel in 1763. The west end of the square is bordered by *Langheim Court,* which has

Obere Karolinenstrasse

a pretty inner courtyard. It was the town residence of the Cistercian monastery of Langheim from 1154–1803. The street narrows to where there was once the main gate to the cathedral fortress. It is known as "Torschuster".

Torschuster

The square on the other side of the gateway extends over the former graveyard of *St. James's Church* (Jakobskirche). Its Baroque façade (by Johann Michael Fischer, 1771, the statue of St. James by Ferdinand Tietz) conceals at a first glance that we are in fact standing in front of the only, still almost purely Romanesque church in Bamberg. It is architecturally so interesting because it is probably a copy of the old cathedral built by Henry: a pillared basilica with a flat roof and two chancels. The eastern one is no longer recognizable from the outside because of the Baroque façade and inside, because of the organ, only if you look closely. The western one was altered to Gothic style. The church was begun for a canonry chapter in 1065 but, after various turmoils, not finished until 1109 by Bishop Otto the Holy. The oldest existent stone coat of arms of the town, the Meranier eagle, is to be found on the tower, put there at the behest of Poppo von Andechs-Meranien, dean of the chapter. Almost nothing remains of the former rich Romanesque and Baroque furnishings. If you are lucky and find the door in the south aisle open, you can catch a glimpse of the idyllic scene of the former chapter buildings.

St. James's Church

Meranier coat of arms

The way to Michelsberg Monastery (about 10 minutes) leads downhill from Torschuster. At the bottom, in front of the Aufseesianum boarding-house for pupils, you come to the fifth of the seven stations of the Cross with a depiction of Christ meeting Veronica (inscription: "Here Christ pressed His holy face into the veil of the woman Veronica in front of her house. VC steps from Pilate's house"). The *way of the Cross* was donated by the rich and childless Heinrich Marschalk von Raueneck around 1500. On a pilgrimage to Jerusalem, he had counted the number of steps from Pilate's house to each of the stations on the way to Calvary and he then transferred these distances to the Bamberg setting. It is the oldest way of the Cross in Germany. It begins in

From St. James's to Michelsberg Monastery

Way of the Cross

44

front of St. Elizabeth's Church and ends at St. Fideo (St. Getreu).

The climb to Michelsberg hill is lined by beautiful Baroque houses and old trees. On the brow of the hill the gateway to the former Benedictine monastery of *Michelsberg* (now a municipal old people's home) opens up. It was founded in 1015, experienced intellectual and economic ascendency in the 12th century, an ascendency which manifested itself in the rich production of its scriptorium among other things. Bishop Otto the Holy gave it special support and he was also buried there in his "favourite resting place" in 1139. The church he built burnt down partly in 1610. When the roof was rebuilt, the post-Gothic

Michelsberg

History of building

Michelsberg Monastery, last resting plae of St. Otto

ceiling vault with its famous *Heavenly Garden* was constructed: over 600 plants painted with botanical exactitude, a monumental book of herbs.

The mediaeval fortified monastery, which can still be seen in the *Panels relating to the Legend of Otto* painted in 1628, was altered completely in the Baroque Age. The brothers Leonhard and Johann Dientzenhofer erected the new monastery buildings between 1696 and 1725 and converted the church to Baroque style. The decorative flight of steps, which leads up to the façade added to the church, is a very popular setting for wedding couples.

Interior furnishings The basic Romanesque character is still noticeable inside the church, but harmonizes well with the Baroque furnishings, which Johann Joseph Scheubel the Elder and Leonhard Gollwitzer worked at as well as other Bamberg Baroque artists. The most beautiful object is the *pulpit*. The joiner Anton Thomas and the carver Georg Reuss created this floating, shimmering something in 1751. The cabinet-maker Servatius Brickard was employed by the monastery. He created his main work, the *choir stalls* with their rich marquetry, around 1730.

Tomb of St. Otto Anyone who suffers from back pains should walk under the raised choir (1725). There stands the *tomb* of St. Otto, a work endowed by Abbot Johann von

Detail from the "Heavenly Garden" on the ceiling of St. Michael's

46

Fuchs around 1440. in a sort of crypt. The gap to slip Michelsberg through gives the believer contact with the saint and his healing powers. The memorial slab on the rear wall is of artistic importance and was made by a Würzburg artist in 1288. It shows Otto, who was almost 80 years old when he died, as a man in his best years, whose charisma is perceptible.

An exceptional jewel is the *Holy Sepulchre Chapel* Holy Sepulchre Chapel (restored 1990/95), which you can enter from the end of the right aisle. The set of scenes of death on the ceiling recall its former function as a burial chamber. The almost unknown stucco reliefs are not only of high artistic quality, they were also conceived with a highly original programme: Death carries off children and old, poor and rich, as is usual in such scenes, but he also blows soap bubbles and reflects on himself while looking at a skull.

10 *monuments* to Bamberg bishops from the 16th to 18th century stand in the side aisles. They were banished from the cathedral during its purification in 1833. The sequence offers a lesson in art history in itself.

The *Brewery Museum* has found a domicile in the Brewery Museum former monastery brewery. Its aim is to display the history of brewing beer.

The terrace behind the monastery church offers an impressive view over the town and the surrounding countryside, from the hills of the Hassberge to Franconian Jura. At the end of the terrace is the beginning of a footpath through the old monastery garden. It ends in Untere Sandstrasse and leads to the coach park by the Regnitz or back to the town centre.

Let us return to Torschuster. From there we go down the hill alongside the wall of the former cathedral fortress into Maternstrasse. Forsythia hangs down over the old stones of the wall. Opposite, the tiny houses, formerly for the canons' servants, nestle into the hill. We pass *Matern Chapel,* home in winter Matern Chapel to an exhibition of Christmas cribs well worth seeing, and come to a crossroads where we can decide between three different ways. The shortest is a path that turns off left through "Domgrund", the valley between cathedral hill and Kaulberg hill, and leads back to the cathedral.

Altenburg Castle

If we turn right, we come to a sign: "Zur *Altenburg*" (to Altenburg Castle) by the next-but-one street to the right. The road up can be recommended only to walkers with good shoes – it is about three kilometres and steep in parts. Drivers can park at a car park below the castle. If you are tired from the climb up, you will be rewarded with a wonderful view over the town and far over the countryside to the Jura and Steiger Forest. The castle, richly-furnished residence of the Bamberg bishops in the 14th and 15th century, was almost completely destroyed by Margrave Albrecht Alcibiades in 1553. The "wild margrave" carried off 400 wagons of silver tableware, gold and jewels, which had been "moved to safety" from ecclesiastical property to the Altenburg, according to the shocked and surely exaggerated report of a Bamberg nun of the order of St. Clare. The present-day castle is largely the result of the Romantic yearning for castles. Dr. Adalbert Friedrich Marcus, the famous doctor, bought the ruined castle in 1801. E.T.A. Hoffmann also belonged to the circle of friends at his festivities in the castle.

Altenburg Society

After the death of Marcus, the newly-founded Altenburg Society was able to catch the Bambergers' enthusiasm for the castle and continue the tedious work of preservation to the present day. The chapel

Altenburg Castle

48

Carmelite cloisters, capital: Mary and St. Theodore, portrayed as a knight, on his knees and with his helmet on his back

was installed in 1834, the palace building finished in 1902. In the mediaeval gateway passage stands the alleged monument to the legendary margrave Adalbert von Babenberg (d. 906). Many people still consider the Altenburg to have been his castle.

From Domgrund the street called "Am Knöcklein" leads up the hill to the *Carmelite Church*. From this side we are met by the west façade of the Romanesque church with its walled-up Lions' Portal. If you want to enter the church, you have to go round the other side of the building, to the end where the chancel used to be. In its place Leonhard Dientzenhofer erected the present façade with Leonhard Gollwitzer's statues in the course of converting the church to Baroque style in 1707. The church belonged to the convent of St. Mary and Theodore, founded by Bishop Eberhard II in 1157. The Carmelites moved into the convent, which had been abandoned meantime, in 1589. The building was secularized in 1803 but they have had possession

49

Upper Parish, the largest Gothic church in the town

Carmelite Church again since 1902. The *Carmelite cloisters* were created by masters of the Parler School of stonemasons in 1392. It is interesting that, at the height of Gothic, they went back to Romanesque forms such as the rounded arches of the arcades. Thus the cloisters are thought to be Romanesque in the eyes of many right up to the present day. A comparison with the remains of the Hohenstaufen convent building, which were discovered during restoration in 1974, reveals however the completely different intellectual world in which the capitals of the cloisters, richly ornamented and often enigmatic, were carved.

Upper Parish Church The greatest building project in Bamberg in the 14th century was the *Upper Parish Church* (Obere Pfarre), the Catholic town parish church of "Our Lady" on the Kaulberg hill. The cathedral chapter (the highest priest was always a cathedral canon) and its worldly relations, but also the townspeople showed their presence, as the keystones in the vaulting show. The ascetic nave was built 1338/1387 and the architecturally magnificent chancel was added from 1392 on. From the valley the chancel seems to float above the roofs like a giant ship. Again we find the forms of the Bohemian Parler School in its rich ornamentation, just as on the church tower. The tower is crowned by the wooden, plastered building of the watchman's lodging. It was intended as only a

50

temporary fixture in 1537, meanwhile it has become a town landmark.

Upper Parish Church

The *Bridal Porch* on the north side of the nave shows the Coronation of Mary in the tympanum (sponsus and sponsa), in the reveals the Wise and Foolish Virgins in fashionable dress of the period around 1350. A stone canopy in front of the portal, which was carved by Bamberg sculptors, protected the wedding party from rain during the marriage ceremony. It took place in front of the door.

Bridal Porch
(ill. p. 13)

In 1711, the stucco master Johann Jakob Vogel began to convert the interior to Baroque style, thereby introducing strapwork to Franconia in this church. Remarkable care was taken with the mediaeval substance. So the Upper Parish Church is the only church in Bamberg that has retained numerous Gothic carvings. The *miraculous statue* of the enthroned Madonna remained as centre of the Baroque high altar (Cologne, around 1330). It is the object of numerous pilgrimages to the Virgin. On the high feast day of the Upper Parish Church (Sunday after the Ascension of Mary) it is dressed in rich Baroque robes and carried in a long procession to the Pietà of St. Martin's.

Miraculous statue

The figures of the 12 *Apostles and the Saviour,* the work of the sculptor Ulrich Widmann in 1481, were set on the pillars of the nave but painted white to fit

12 Apostles and Saviour

Upper Parish, ambulatory: Anna Lying In (around 1500)

the Baroque furnishings. The ambulatory kept its Gothic appearance. The *tabernacle,* dated 1392, is in one of the niches. The front shows the Burial of Christ at the bottom, the Apostles in the middle, the Last Judgment in the surmount. In the next niche is a moving scene of *Anna Lying In* (around 1500): Anna holds the completely swaddled infant pressed lovingly to her, while Joachim has fallen asleep exhausted at the foot of the bed. Between the ambulatory and the right aisle stands the remarkable *font.* It has a rare depiction of the seven sacraments on wooden panels which cover the stone pedestal. They were made by a Bamberg carver around 1515. His mark was a predilection for a wealth of tiny, lovingly
carved details. Two reliefs showing *Ascension* and *Coronation of Mary,* which hang on the wall of the right aisle, came from the late-mediaeval high altar and were made in Bamberg around 1500. There is a striking difference to the magnificent painting by Jacopo Tintoretto with the same theme hanging next to them: *Mary is received into Heaven.* Only about 50 years lie between the two works of art, but a completely new conception of art came to Bamberg with the Venetian's work. The important cathedral dean, Johann Christoph Neustetter, known as Stormer, had bought the picture, that was revolutionary for its time even in Venice, and left it to the cathedral. It was set into an altar there in 1651. Since 1937 it has hung in the Upper Parish Church, a loan in exchange for the Veit Stoss altar.

The *New Ebrach Court,* built by the town architect Martin Mayer in 1765, lies opposite the church. It belonged to the prosperous monastery of Ebrach,
which also had the *Old Ebrach Court* (1682) at its disposal as a second town residence. Its mighty late-Renaissance gable overlooks the Vorderer Bach street.

Behind the chancel of Upper Parish Church we come into the Eisgrube street, from where we should take another look back, and then left into Juden-
strasse (Jewry Street). A large Jewish community lived there from the 12th century on. In the course of the Middle Ages, they were by turns tolerated and persecuted. There does not seem to have been a real

Upper Parish, side aisle, Jacopo Tintoretto: Mary is received into Heaven (1547/48)

pogrom as in other towns as a result of the great plague in 1348. But from about 1420 onwards, life was made so difficult for the Jews that they gradually moved away. The synagogue, situated at the end of Judenstrasse in the Pfahlplätzchen square, was converted into a *Lady chapel,* like in other places. It is now used by the Baptists.

Former synagogue

The splendid *Böttinger House* rises massively from the confined space of Judenstrasse. The richest of ornamentation shows even outside the high standard that its nouveau riche builder called for. Ignaz Tobias Böttinger, a high-ranking civil servant under Prince

Böttinger House

53

Bishop Lothar Franz von Schönborn, had this first bourgeois town "palais" built between 1708 and 1713. It is still a question of dispute as to who the architect was. Presumably Böttinger made the dreams, which his "grand tour" through Italy had inspired, come true in this house with the help of the town architect Andreas Ammon. The problem of an extremely awkward site at the foot of the steep Stephansberg hill has been skillfully managed: one can step out onto one of the terraces of the garden from each floor of the rear wings. On the other hand there are certain violations of the architectural theories of the time and by the time it was finished the house was already a little old-fashioned. Apart from that, an open stairwell is most charming in an

Böttinger House, Ignaz Tobias Böttinger's first town "palais" (1708/13)

54

Italian palazzo, less so in the severe Bamberg winter, and rooms "en filant", leading from one to the other without corridors, were rather unpractical in a household with 12 children like Böttinger's.

Just three years after Böttinger House was finished, the court counsellor therefore began building a second palace. It is called *Concordia;* the name comes from a townspeople's society that filled it with social gatherings in the 19th century. Today it is seat of the Geochemical Institute. During working hours it is possible to ring the bell and see into the stairwell with its stucco by J. J. Vogel. The stairwell demonstrates Böttinger's wish for progressive architecture with its turning to elegant French Baroque and the separation of private and reception rooms. Böttinger by then belonged to the "Establishment" and was able to afford the engagement of the prince bishop's architect. Johann Dietzenhofer erected the two-winged building with a façade overlooking the river in the years 1716 to 1722. He was influenced by that miracle of a work that was just being built in Pommersfelden, Weissenstein Palace for Prince Bishop Lothar Franz von Schönborn.

St. Stephen's Church lies diagonally above Concordia. According to legend, St. Kunigunde paid for the building, as is to be seen in the relief on the imperial tomb in the cathedral. In 1020 it was consecrated by none less than Pope Benedict VIII, who happened to be in Bamberg just then at the famous "summit conference" with Emperor Henry II. Nothing remains of that church. The oldest part of the present church is the 13th-century tower. A new church was begun with the chancel by Giovanni Bonalino in 1626, but it could not be completed due to the Thirty Years' War. Only when the economic situation had improved somewhat was it possible to commission Antonio Petrini, the "father of Main-Franconian Baroque", to continue in 1677. A west wing with a remarkable façade, even if visible only from a few spots, and a transept together with the chancel form a cross with equal arms. The Greek cross plan would have shown more clearly if the planned dome had been realized, but the money ran out. The opening in the crossing was provisionally closed with a stucco

Concordia

Stairwell

St. Stephen's
Church

relief that portrays the martyrdom of Stephen and was made by Johann Jakob Vogel in 1688. The church, which had been secularized and stripped of all its furnishings, was put at the disposal of the Bamberg Protestant community in 1808. The interior was restored in 1987 and the uniformly white decoration has enhanced the effect of light and space in St. Stephen's. The new altar furnishings by Jürgen Görz (1986) are somewhat daring, provoking some serious consideration.

Round the church lie the courts of the former canons: in a dominating situation above the valley, the "House of the Golden Arms" (No. 1 Oberer Stephansberg), dating from 1615. Behind St.

Stephen's the narrow, steep street, Eisgrube, leads back to Upper Parish Church. The bulbous face on the door knob of house No. 14 Eisgrube was the

model for the Apple Woman in E.T.A. Hoffmann's "Golden Pot".

Sandstrasse at the foot of the cathedral hill was the area where the first Bamberg town settlement grew

up. The church of the *Dominican Monastery,* founded by Bishop Wulfing von Stubenberg in 1310, was erected on the site of the former town court. Only the carved figure of Christopher above the portal, the work of Ulrich Widmann around 1480, shows that the church was dedicated to St. Christopher. In Bamberg it is now known under the name "Chamber of Culture"; until 1993 it was home to the

Bamberg Symphony Orchestra. It is possible to see the Dominican cloisters. The Dominican monastery, dissolved like all the monasteries in the principality during secularization, was converted into administrative offices in 1985.

Two late-Gothic vaulted rooms of the former monastery are a very popular place to go to, for Bambergers as well as tourists: they are the inn

rooms of the *Schlenkerla* brewery, where the famous smoked beer is tapped. Allegedly it does not taste until you have had at least two glasses, but then it is unforgettable. Schlenkerla gets its name from a landlord in the 19th century: "because he dangled his arms a bit, that's why we christened him Little Dangler (Schlenkerla) out of sheer high spirits and mockery", a chronicle reports in local dialect. Nowadays Sandstrasse is the centre of Bamberg's "night life". It has a whole host of restaurants and pubs and this has caused the town council to forbid the opening of any more to the benefit of the people who live there.

The steep climb up Untere Karolinenstrasse, which leads the visitor to the majestic expanse of the cathedral square, is of particular architectural finesse. This effect was planned purposely in the Baroque Age. Thus the portal of *Bibra House* (No. 11 Untere Karolinenstrasse, 1716) takes up and quotes the forms of the Residence portal. Diagonally

Untere Karolinenstrasse

Bibra House

57

opposite stands *Marschalk von Ostheim House.* Astonishingly, it retained its half-timbered gable, a horror for the Baroque Age. To redress this, it has a remarkable Baroque stairwell with a painted trompe l'œil cupola (around 1720; usually closed). The *Court Pharmacy,* one of the oldest pharmacies in Germany, its core dating back to a 1455 building, was altered by Erasmus Braun in 1577 and once again in the Baroque Age. The "Coronation of Mary" (around 1750) on the corner of the building emphasizes the ranking of a building in the street leading to the cathedral square.

The Old Town Hall in the middle of the river, linking the two parts of the bourgeois town (1453/1755)

Bourgeois Town between the Arms of the Regnitz

A very unusual building stands at the start of our tour of "bourgeois" Bamberg: a town hall in the middle of the river must be unique in Germany. According to legend, the Bamberg citizens built it on a specially made island in the left arm of the Regnitz because the bishop refused to give them one inch of land. This is reminiscent of the fight between the bishop and the townspeople over power in the town. A decisive factor for the location of the *Old Town Hall* must have been however its function as a link between the first town settlement in the Sand district and the new "quarter" on the island, which gained in importance from the 12th century on. The core of the town hall goes back to a 1453 building (Gothic vaulting under the archway), but it was altered by the town architect Martin Mayer in Baroque times. A façade was added to both sides of the three-storeyed mediaeval tower on the *Upper Bridge*. Bonaventura Mutschele, the most talented of the great Bamberg family of sculptors, designed the Rococo balconies in 1755 and the coats of arms above them: facing the hill, the town coat of arms, the town knight with the eagle shield (original in Geyerswörth Castle courtyard), facing the valley, the coat of arms of the prince bishop, Franz Konrad von Stadion (1753–1757). Johann Anwander created the paintings on the long fronts – allegories of the virtues sovereigns possess – in 1755. They were restored in 1960. The half-timbering of the so-called Rottmeisterhäuschen (1668) was restored to its original colourfulness in 1980. Since 1995 the Old Town Hall has housed the Ludwig Porcelain and Faïence Collection, exquisite Baroque pieces, above all Meissen and Strasbourg.

Over the middle pillar of the bridge stands the mighty *Crucifixion group,* which the court engineer, J. F. Rosenzweig, commissioned from Johann Leonhard Gollwitzer in 1715. Opposite it, just past the statue of St. John Nepomuk, you have an unforgettable view of the steeply soaring chancel of the Upper Parish Church.

To the north the Old Town Hall is flanked by the

Upper Bridge

Old Town Hall

Town coat of arms

Crucifixion group

59

Lower Bridge. Created by Balthasar Neumann in 1739 and often rebuilt, it was blown up, like all the Bamberg bridges, at the end of the Second World War. It was replaced by an unimaginative concrete slab in 1967. Kunigunde looks down on it with a smile. She is the last of five monumental sandstone figures made by Peter Benkert in 1743, a statue "in which elemental strength wonderfully mingles with the charm of Rococo" (a copy made 1992). She turns her back on one of the picture postcard views of Bamberg: the picturesque line of fishermen's houses with their high roofs and half-timbering, wooden balconies, tiny gardens by the river, flat boats and nets spread out, and the equally picturesque name of *"Little Venice"*.

Geyerswörth Castle lies a few metres upstream on an island. The Geyers were one of the rich patrician families that left the town after the Immunity War of 1435. The principality purchased their castle and it was rebuilt, except for the tower, as residence for the prince bishop by Asmus Braun in 1586. The coat of arms above the gate into the courtyard betrays who had it built: Prince Bishop Ernst von Mengersdorf (1583–1591). The frescoes of the Seven Free Arts in the splendidly painted *Renaissance Chamber* tell of the bishop's learning. Since the room was restored in 1984, it has served as a reception chamber for the town of Bamberg. The original town coat of arms from the Old Town Hall was set up in a protected spot in one of the arcades of the courtyard. There is an enchanting view over the whole of the Old Town from the tower (key from the Tourist Office in wing overlooking the castle garden).

At the rear of Geyerswörth Castle the half-moon arch of a footbridge spans the old *Ludwig-Danube-Main Canal*. A favourite project of King Ludwig I of Bavaria, that from the beginning suffered competition from the railway, it was begun in Kelheim in 1836 and came to an end after the 100th lock by the old harbour in Bamberg. This spot named *Kranen* (= crane). north of the Lower Bridge, was once the focal point of river traffic: the boats were loaded and unloaded with the help of the iron cranes which are still there, goods were transferred, the fishermen offered their catch for sale. The smell there must

"Little Venice", the houses of the fishermen and boatmen

have been fantastic, for the town *slaughterhouse* also stood here. In the gable of the old slaughterhouse of 1742 (now a university faculty library) a stone ox is stolidly ensconced. The somewhat puzzling Latin inscription says it was never a calf, but created straightaway as a full-grown ox by the artist J. A. Nickel. The east side of the square is dominated by the *Wedding House*. The townspeople could rent rooms and hire servants for their festivities in the house, which was built by the town in Renaissance style in 1603. It is one of the buildings that was quite heavily damaged in the Second World War. It was restored in a somewhat simpler fashion and is now part of the Bamberg university.

Slaughterhouse

Wedding House

Past Obstmarkt (fruit market) we come to the main marketplace of the town, *Grüner Markt* (green market), which means the vegetable market. In addition there are still the squares called Heumarkt, Holzmarkt and Obstmarkt (hay, timber and fruit markets); there also used to be a sow, fish and corn market and others. Holding markets was one of the most important rights and actual functions of the town. Grüner Markt became centre of the bourgeois settlement developing around it from the 12th century onwards and has remained so until the present day. It now forms the central part of the pedestrian precinct, whose dubious "furnishings" are being changed bit by bit. During the day there is generally a milling mass of tourists and local people, shoppers in a hurry, window-shoppers and those who enjoy an ice cream and the sunshine in a street café.

Grüner Markt

Markets

Pedestrian precinct

61

The mighty façade of *St. Martin's Church* forms a dignified contrast. It was the Jesuit church "In the Name of Jesus". In 1611 the Jesuits had taken over the former Carmelite monastery, whose church looked towards Austrasse. In 1686, after they had been able to buy a large enough site in the market-place, they began building a new church in accordance with the spirit of the Counter-Reformation. To this end they sent for Georg Dientzenhofer from Prague, head of one of the new building firms with a large staff that no longer kept to guild restrictions. After Georg's death, his brother Leonhard took over direction of building. The "firm" completed the

The "Fork Man" in front of the façade of St. Martin's

gigantic building in seven years. It was with this success that the Dientzenhofer Era of Franconian Baroque began, from which the New Residence, the monasteries of Banz, Ebrach and Michelsberg, the Pommersfelden palace and many other buildings stem – a climax in not only Franconian but also European art history. After secularization, the function of the old market church, which stood on the present-day Maxplatz square and was pulled down in 1804, as well as its patron saint, were transferred to the former Jesuit church, which has been the main parish church of the town ever since. Some of the works of art of the old St. Martin's were saved and installed in this church, most important of all the *Pietà* on the right side altar. It was made in Cologne around 1330 and is one of the earliest so-called "joyous Vesper Images": Mary holds her dead Son on her lap, smiling because she recognizes redemption in His Passion. The so-called *"Mortal Agony Panels"*, carved portrayals of Christ's Passion, were created with the works of Dürer as model (1511). The austere interior of the church is dominated by the theatrical and sumptuous wall of the *high altar,* a work in stucco marble by the Italian Giovanni B. Brenno (1701). The *illusory dome* over the crossing, painted by Francesco Marchini, copying Andrea Pozzo, in 1714, was the first of this kind in Germany. After restoration of the church in 1984, it shows to better advantage.

The buildings of the former *Jesuit College* adjoin St. Martin's. They are grouped round a courtyard under the shade of an enormous and rare tree, a black walnut. It is a place of restful quiet right in the middle of the turbulence of the town centre, and that even though the buildings are now part of the university. The rooms of the old university library are still in use.

At the right end of the north wing the *Natural History Museum* hides itself. One of the oldest museums in Germany, it receives more and more attention. Prince Bishop Franz Ludwig von Erthal had it established in 1795, completely in accordance with the spirit of Enlightenment "for the benefit of the whole population". The collections include con-

St. Martin's Church

Franconian Baroque

Pietà

Mortal Agony Panels

High altar

Illusory dome

Jesuit College

Natural History Museum

63

served animals, some of them already extinct, fossils, minerals and so on. The classicist furnishings, which have been preserved, are actually in themselves a museum within a museum.

The Jesuit college flanks the street called "An der Universität". This new name for the former Jesuiten-strasse shows that we are now in the university quarter. The Bamberg university was refounded in 1979 and integrated into the Old Town. It makes use of a large number of historical buildings situated between the Regnitz and Grüner Markt, including the so-called *Aula,* remains of the former Jesuit school building. Only the Renaissance portal dating from 1612 serves to recall the time of its origin. Today it is used as a university faculty library.

Grüner Markt, which was domicile of the rich Bamberg merchant families from the beginning, was deliberately planned in the Baroque Age, its architecture worked out to the last detail. Upper-class Baroque houses set the tone. The Neptune Fountain sets an important accent. The Bambergers call him
"Gabelmann" (Fork Man), because he holds a three-pronged trident in his hand. Prince Bishop Lothar Franz von Schönborn first made the sculptor, Kaspar Metzner, construct a full-size wooden model of the fountain in 1698. Thus they ascertained the optimal position for it to fit into the spatial lines of the square. To what extent our modern times have forgotten how to see with an awareness for spatial effects is shown by the fact that the fountain lost its socle, was heaped up with stones and encumbered with two trees when the pedestrian precinct was made.

The square *Maxplatz* connects to Grüner Markt in the direction of the right arm of the Regnitz. The square was created by the demolition of the old St. Martin's Church in 1804. It is enclosed on the right and the left by the spacious Baroque buildings of the old *priests' seminary* and the former *St. Catherine's Spital.* They were built according to plans by Baltha-sar Neumann from 1729/38. St. Catherine's Spital owed its origins to a 1203 endowment by the patrician family Tockler. Prince Bishop Friedrich Karl von Schönborn intended it to bring all the spitals in the town together. It is now used as a private dwelling

64

and as part of a department store. The seminary was turned into the New Town Hall in 1928, after a new priests' seminary had been built in the Hain area. New Town Hall Maxplatz is where the daily vegetable market is held with produce from the Bamberg market-gardeners – Vegetable market it is a pleasure just to look at the piles of vegetables and fruit. The square was named after the Bavarian king, Max I Joseph. Surrounded by the saints Henry, Kunigunde and Otto and King Konrad III, he stands on the pillar of the *Maximilian Fountain,* a work made by Ferdinand von Miller in 1888.

Hauptwachstrasse, leading on from Maxplatz, is named after the former main guardhouse. The build- Hauptwach-strasse ing, designed by the court military counsellor, J. G. Roppelt, in 1772, now houses a baker's shop, watched over by martial-looking stone guards by J. B. Kamm.

From here we can turn into *Promenade*. It was part Promenade of the town moat until it was filled in with material cleared from the cathedral square in 1776 and, on the orders of the prince bishop, Adam Friedrich von Seinsheim, planted with an avenue of trees, to give the townspeople the chance to take a restful walk. Nowadays that is hardly possible, as it is now a large car park and the central bus station.

The south end of Promenade runs into *Lange* Lange Strasse *Strasse.* It is one of the town's main shopping streets and, in spite of some new buildings, a unified en- semble of prestigious town houses, in particular of the 18th century. The late-Gothic *Haus zum Saal* (also known as Wallenstein House, Nr. 3 Lange Strasse) stands out especially. Its façade was altered to Baroque style and is watched over by a charming Immaculata by Leonhard Gollwitzer (1715) above the portal.

The tiny Habergasse opposite leads to *Zinken-* Zinkenwörth *wörth.* In the Middle Ages, this was a quarter with its own jurisdiction and known for its alert, rebellious spirit. This is where the Bamberg uprising during the Peasants' Revolt originated, it was here that the pamphlets of the Reformation were printed. Nowa- days we mainly think back to the Romantic Age here. The municipal theatre, built 1808, stands in *Schillerplatz*. In the same year E.T.A. Hoffmann Schillerplatz took up a position as director of music, but had to resign it a short time later. After that he carried out all sorts of different jobs in the theatre, all of them deplorably paid. He lived in the tiny, narrow-fronted house opposite until 1813. It now contains a museum in his memory.

E.T.A. Hoffmann Museum

Past the former municipal police prison (now home of Stadtbau, the municipal buildings office), we come to *Schönleinsplatz*. The quarters of planned expansion of the town in the 19th century begin from here. Willy Lessing Strasse provided the link to the east, to the station. Rich Bamberg industrialists and merchants, including many Jewish hop merchants, used to live in the street as also in Hainstrasse. Both streets are still almost unified ensembles of late-classicist and end-of-the-century villas; some of them still have the buildings behind which always belonged to them – the small factory buildings, the warehouses of their trade. The removal of the trees and the heavy traffic have certainly spoilt the "atmosphere" in Willy Lessing Strasse, so that only Hainstrasse still has visible traces of the builders' self-importance and wealth. One of the most magnificent houses, the *Villa Dessauer* (Nr. 4 a Hainstrasse), was built for the hop merchant, Carl Emanuel Dessauer, by the Hanover architect, F. Geb, in 1883. It was restored in 1987 and made into the Municipal Art Gallery. The *State Archives* at the south end of Hainstrasse are in a 1905 neo-Baroque building.

Schönleinsplatz

Hainstrasse

Villa Dessauer

State Archives

Hain Park

The adjoining park, called *Hain,* was laid out on the orders of the Bavarian king by Stephan Freiherr von Stengel in 1803. The English Garden in Munich was the model. Instead of the wild, marshy woods there before, a "naturally arranged" park grew up with gently curving paths and wonderful clusters of old trees, with a little temple and a bandstand, various monuments and a Botanical Garden. It spreads over the whole south tip of the island between the two arms of the Regnitz.

The right arm of the Regnitz was converted into part of the Rhine-Main-Danube Canal. A path along the bank leads past the priests' seminary, built in 1927, back to the town. On the way one comes to *Wilhelmsplatz*. The whole square was planned by the municipal building counsellor, Hans Jakob Erlwein,

Wilhelmsplatz

66

"Druids' Temple" under the modern Hain Bridge in the Hain park

who left a decisive mark on building in Bamberg around 1900. One side is lined by the Law Courts, **Law Courts** built by Max Höfl in 1903, the then Upper Postal Head Office of 1905 stands opposite. The synagogue built by Johannes Kronfuss in 1910 bordered the third side of the square. It was destroyed in the so-called "Crystal Night" in 1938. The 1995 memorial by J. Bandau in nearby Synagogue Square calls for earnest reflection on the Jews' fate.

In the period of industrial expansion from 1871 on, ("Gründerzeit"), the town grew in the north. The former maternity hospital in Weide square was converted into a university building in 1990. The concert and congress hall, opened in 1993, rises from the banks of the river. The *Old Hospital* opposite, built **Old** by Prince Bishop Franz Ludwig von Erthal in 1789, **Hospital** then most modern hospital in Europe (architect: Johann Lorenz Fink), is now a hotel. The old surgery building at the town end, built by Hans J. Erlwein in 1901, now houses the Municipal Archives.

Market-gardeners' Town: Theuerstadt and East Bamberg

The areas of the town east of the right arm of the Regnitz are not perhaps as photogenic as the grand hill district or the bourgeois town on the island, but they are of equal importance for the structure of the town. The ancient long-distance trade route, which began in Lübeck and stretched through the whole of the mediaeval empire to Regensburg, ran through this area. The road today has taken on many names as it passes through Bamberg: Hallstadter Strasse, Siechenstrasse, Königstrasse, Nürnberger Strasse; the part called Steinweg (= paved road) recalls its importance, just as the numerous breweries and inns, which established themselves along it, do. Their wrought-iron brackets and inn signs are a chapter of arts and crafts in itself.

St. Gangolf's is the spiritual centre of the district, focal point of the Theuerstadt quarter. Founded as a canonry church in 1058, it has been the parish church since secularization. The original 11th century building still survives in the exterior walls, although it was altered frequently. The solid twin towers, begun in late-Romanesque style under Bishop Otto the Holy, were altered to Gothic around 1400 and given their symbol-like onion tops in 1671. Only the *high altar*, the *choir stalls* and the effervescent *altars* in the side chapels still testify to the magnificence of the Baroque furnishings. They are all works by the Mutschele family, who lived near St. Gangolf's and for whom the furnishing of their "home church" was more than just a job. The neo-Gothic furnishings, which had superseded the Baroque around 1850, were in turn replaced by works of art from other Bamberg churches in 1938. B. Kamm made the *pulpit* for the chapel of St. Catherine's Spital in 1786. The moving *crucifix of branches* from the 14th century in the left transept came from the old St. Martin's Church. The *Madonna on the Crescent Moon* (after 1508) used to stand in the Franciscan church, which was demolished in 1807. The *Holy Mass Altar*, consecrated in 1978, is the work of Paul Schinner. A crucified Christ, in regal robes and crowned, hangs in

Mediaeval long-distance trade route

St. Gangolf's in Theuerstadt

Mutschele family of sculptors

the *Chapel of Divine Aid.* It goes back to the original model of the Volto Santo in Lucca, of whom many copies were mistaken for St. Liberata, The legend tells that she did not want to marry her betrothed, a heathen, and, in answer to her prayers, she grew a beard. Thereupon her incensed father had her nailed to the cross. The Divine Aid crucifix came from the Convent of the Holy Sepulchre and is a copy of the crucifix donated by Frank Münzmeister (d. 1356).

Franz Münzmeister and his wife were the founders of the *Holy Sepulchre Convent,* which they endowed in honour of Christ's grave after returning from a pilgrimage to the Holy Land. After secularization only the church remained, profaned and robbed of its furnishings. Dominican nuns returned in 1926 and built a small new convent.

St. Gangolf's, north side

69

Market-
gardening
district

Liquorice

Market-
gardeners'
and Wine-
growers'
Museum

East Bamberg

The convent lies in the middle of the old market-gardening district. From the 13th century Bamberg patrician families began to invest their capital in a special form of cultivation: growing vegetables on land between Hauptsmoor Forest and the right arm of the Regnitz. The smallholder townsmen they brought to Bamberg to do so were so successful that vegetables, but above all liquorice and seeds, became an important export and economic factor for the town. Originally the smallholdings were isolated but then grew together in long rows. The houses were given large gateways to drive through to the fields which lay behind. This structure of house still remains in some streets, as for example in Mittel-strasse. There the *Market-gardeners' and Wine-growers' Museum* endearingly displays the customs and way of life of this very original trade, together with those of the "Häcker", the dialect name for the wine-growers on the hills.

The market-gardening district was cut into two by the railway line in the 19th century. Luitpoldstrasse from the station to the town centre was driven right through houses and fields. The whole of the residential and industrial area east of the railway line, known as East Bamberg, was built on market-gardening fields. The remaining fields, near the centre and desirable housing sites, are also endangered.

The market-gardeners' religious centre was *St.*

Market-garden-ers' and Wine-growers' Museum in a typical small-holder's house

Sebastian's Chapel, which was saved from demolition after secularization and again in 1984, thanks to initiatives on the part of townspeople, including many market-gardeners (Siechenstrasse; not open to the public). The former *infirmary for incurables* stands next to it and has been converted into a savings bank. *St. Otto's Church* is a remarkable building by Otto Orlando Kurz, 1914. Michael Kurz completed *St. Henry's Church* in East Bamberg in 1929. The *Church of Our Redeemer* stands on Kunigundendamm. It was built in the form of a Greek cross by German Bestelmeyer in 1933. The parish church, dedicated to Mary, in the *Wunderburg* district at the end of Kunigundendamm was conceived as a neo-Gothic hall church by Chrysostomus Martin in 1889. In this area there are breweries, too, where you can recover from the tiring art tours.

And that is what you should do, because it is something typical of Bamberg. This is a town to get to know with all your senses. If you approach it only with your intellect, you will never understand it. The blaze of colour of the processions is as much a part of Bamberg as the flavour of the different beers, the world-famous Bamberg Symphony just as much as the church hymns, the contrary humour just as the stubborn pride of the citizens in their town. A town where you can live well, whether as a visitor or as a local, and a town where, with open eyes, you can find things to dream about.

St. Sebastian's Chapel

Incurables' infirmary

St. Otto's Church

St. Henry's Church of Our Redeemer

Wunderburg

Wrought-iron inn sign of the "Spezial" brewery in Obere Königstrasse

Information in Brief

Information *Tourist Office,* Geyerswörthstrasse 3, Tel. 09 51 / 87 11 61, Post Box 11 01 53. 96033 Bamberg. Agency for hotel rooms and bookings, brochures, guided tours and excursions, organization of conferences. List of hotels, inns, boarding houses, conference rooms, restaurants and cafés

Bamberg Ticket Agency (BVD), Lange Strasse 22, Tel. 09 51 / 98 08 20. Advance sale of tickets for theatre, concerts and other events

ADAC Automobile club, office: Schützenstrasse 4 a, Tel. 2 10 77; Breakdown service: Tel. 1 92 11

Bicycle hire Dratz Bicycles, Pödeldorfer Strasse 190, Tel. 1 24 28. Station (from express goods office), Tel. enquiries 83 23 52

Boat trips F. Kropf, Kapuzinerstrasse 5, Tel. 2 66 79. Round-the-harbour trips, depart from "Am Kranen", see board for times, mid-March to November

Bus service 28 municipal bus routes from bus station (Promenade) to all parts of the town and sights, see timetable (Tel. enquiries 7 71)
The Franken joint bus service (OVF) runs connections to Bayreuth, Coburg, Ebrach, Pommersfelden, Schlüsselfeld and other destinations (Tel. enquiries 3 38 16).

Calendar of events

"Rosenmontag":	(Mon. preceding Shrove Tues.). Rosenmontag Ball in E.T.A. Hoffmann Theatre and Harmonie Rooms
Shrove Tuesday:	Carnival fun in the pedestrian precinct from 1 p.m. on
May:	Spring fair
June:	Franconian Wine Festival Wildensorg church fair St. Otto's church fair
June/July:	Calderón Festival in courtyard of Old Court Serenade concerts in the Rose Garden
July:	University's Old Town Festival Market-gardeners' and Wine-growers' Festival St. Henry's church fair St. Henry's Feast Day Wunderburg church fair
August:	Gartenstadt church fair Laurenzi church fair Sand church fair
October:	Gaustadt church fair Autumn fair
December:	Crib tour and crib exhibitons

Camping In Bug district of town (4 km. from centre), can be reached via Nuremberg road (B 4) and Würzburg road (B 22). Tel. 5 63 20

Car hire *InterRent,* Egelseestraße 72, Tel. 20 29 20

Concerts see BVD
Organ recitals in cathedral: May 1 to October 31, every Saturday, 12–12.30 p.m.

Emergencies
110   Assault, traffic accidents etc.   112   Fire
1 92 22 First aid, ambulance service, night chemists

Guided tours Daily (except Suns. and public holidays) at 2 p.m. Apply for tickets at Tourist Office, Geyerswörthstr. 3, Tel. 87 11 61, adults DM 6,–, pupils DM 3,– Advance booking for parties.
Tours of the cathedral hill (cathedral, Diocesan Museum, New Residence, History Museum, Old Court): apply ticket office, New Residence, Tel. 5 63 51. Adults DM 3,–, parties of 20 and over, pupils and Senior Citizens DM 2,–

73

Lost property Town Hall, Maxplatz, Tel. 87 12 68; open Mon. to Fri., 9–12 a.m.

Markets Fruit and vegetable market: daily, Maxplatz

Flower market: daily, Grüner Markt

Honey market: Shrove Tuesday morning, Maxplatz

Mid-Lent market: wooden articles and basketware, seeds and agricultural articles. Held in middle of Lent between Ash Wednesday and Easter, Grüner Markt and Maxplatz

Spring market: second half of May, Maxplatz (closed Suns.).

Autumn market: second half of October, Maxplatz (closed Suns.)

All Saints' flower market: October 30 and November 1, Siechenstrasse, by entrance to old cemetery, and in Gundelsheimer Strasse

Christmas tree market: December 15–23, Maxplatz, Laurenziplatz, Heinrich Weber Platz and in Gartenstadt

Christmas market: December 1–23, Maxplatz

Municipal offices Town Hall, Maxplatz, switchboard Tel. 87-0, doorman Tel. 87-10 18

Newspaper Fränkischer Tag, Gutenbergstrasse 1, Tel. 18 80

Open-air festival *Calderón Festival* in courtyard of Old Court

Parking *Park-and-ride car park* (buses depart every 10 minutes): Alter Plärrerplatz in south of town (on Rhein-Main-Donau Damm – continuation of Heinrichsdamm)

Car parks: Neuer Plärrerplatz in east of town in Breitenau area (between Memmelsdorfer Strasse and Berliner Ring) Weide (approach via Hornthalstrasse)

Schützenstraße multi-storey (corner of Friedrichstrasse)

Geyerswörth underground car park (Geyerswörthstrasse)

Georgendamm underground car park (by Löwenbrücke)

Residenzschloss underground car park, Untere Sandstrasse

Atrium multi-storey (next to railway station)

Post *Main post office,* Ludwigstrasse 25 (opposite station), Tel. 83 62 88. Monday to Friday, 7 a.m. – 7 p.m.; Saturday, 7 a.m. – 2 p.m.; Sunday, 11 a.m. – 1 p.m.

Railway station *Travel enquiries, Tel. 1 94 19*

Swimming pools *Indoor pool,* Margaretendamm 5, Tel. 87-17 81; *Open-air:* Stadionbad, Tel. 87-17 95 and Gaustadt, Tel. 87-17 93

Taxis Main ranks: station, Promenadenstrasse and (from 7 p.m. only) Grüner Markt. Tel 1 50 15, 3 45 45, 1 94 10, Taxi pilot service Tel. 1 50 18

Theatre E.T.A. Hoffmann Theatre, Schillerplatz 7, Tel. 87-14 33

"Bamberg Calderón Festival", open-air performances in Old Court, June and July

Tickets Advance bookings see BVD

University, Central administration, Kapuzinerstr. 16, Tel. 8 63-1

Youth hostel "Wolfsschlucht", Oberer Leinritt 7 (near Bug), Tel. 5 60 02, closed December 15 – January 31

Opening times

Böttinger House (p. 53), Judenstrasse 14, courtyard only on view

Carmelite Cloisters (p. 50), Karmelitenplatz 1, Tel. 9 52 90. Weekdays from 8.30–11.30 a.m. and 2.30–5.30 p.m., Sundays from 8.30–11 a.m. and 2.30–5 p.m.

Cathedral (p. 27), 1. 5. – 31. 10., 9.30 a.m. – 6 p.m., (in winter to 5 p.m.) No tours during services and on June 29/30. Guided tours: 10.30 a. m., 2 and 5 p. m., Sundays 1 p. m. only (ticket-office in cloisters, Tel. 50 23 30).

Diocesan Museum (p. 38), Domplatz 5, Tel. 50 23 29. Daily: 10 a.m. – 5p.m. (closed Mondays), guided tours: 11 a.m. and 3 p.m. Entrance charges: adults DM 2,–, young people DM 1,–, pupils DM –,50

Dr. Remeis Observatory, Astronomical Institute of Erlangen-Nuremberg University, Sternwartstrasse 7, Tel. 5 77 08. Apply for visits, only weekdays. Entrance charges: adults DM 2,–, pupils DM 1,–

E.T.A. Hoffmann House (p. 66), Schillerplatz 26. Guided tours (E.T.A. Hoffmann House and Mark House) lasting 1 hour from May 7 to October 31, Saturday, 12–1 p.m. (charge DM 5,– per head), for parties Saturday, 1–4 p.m. (charge DM 80,–). Tel. 2 81 73

Franconian Brewery Museum (p. 47), Michelsberg 10 f, Tel. 5 30 16. April 1 to October 31, Thursday to Sunday 1–4 p.m. From November to March by appointment only, phone Otto Metzner (Tel. 6 41 29). Entrance charges: adults DM 3,–, pupils DM 2,–

Geyerswörth Castle, tower (p. 60). Key can be obtained from Tourist office, 9 a.m. – 4 p.m.

History Museum (p. 40), Domplatz 7, Tel. 87-11 42. May 1 to October 31, daily (except Monday) from 9 a.m. – 5 p.m. Entrance charges: adults DM 2,–, parties and young people DM 1,–. Special exhibitions from November 1 to April 30, otherwise closed

Market-gardeners' and Wine-growers' Museum (p. 70), Mittelstrasse 34. May 1 to October 31, Wednesday and Sunday from 2–5 p.m.; parties also by appointment, phone Herr Oswald, Tel. 3 14 77

Missionary Museum in Bug, Schlossstrasse 30, Tel. 5 62 14. Sunday and public holidays from 2–5 p.m. or by tel. appointment. Entrance free

Municipal Archives (p. 67), Untere Sandstrasse 30 a, Tel. 87-13 71. Monday to Wednesday from 8 a.m. – 4 p.m., Thursday 8 a.m. – 8 p.m., Friday 8 a.m. – 2.30 p.m.

Museum for Early-Islamic Art, Austr. 29. Open by appointment only, Tel. 8 63 21 82 (Chair of Turkish Studies, University of Bamberg)

Natural History Museum (p. 63), Fleischstrasse 2, Tel. 8 63 12 48. Daily (except Monday): April 1 to September 30, 9 a.m. – 5 p.m., October 1 to March 31, 10 a.m. – 4 p.m. Entrance charges: adults DM 3,–, children and young people DM 1,50

New Residence (p. 40), Domplatz 8, Tel. 5 63 51. Daily from 9–12 a.m. and 1.30–5 p.m. (from 1. 10. to 31. 3. only to 4 p.m.). Entrance charges: Residence and art gallery DM 3,–. Parties, pupils and Senior Citizens DM 2,–, school classes free

Old Town Hall (p. 59), Ludwig Baroque Porcelain and Faïence Collection. Tel. 87 11 42. Daily (except Monday)

from 9.30 a. m. – 4.30 p. m. Entrance charges: DM 6,–, Senior Citizens, young people DM 4,–.

State Archives (p. 66), Hainstrasse 39, Tel. 2 68 61. Monday from 8.15 a.m. – 4 p.m., Tuesday and Thursday from 8 a.m. – 4 p.m., Wednesday 8 a.m. – 8 p.m., Friday 8 a.m. – 1.30 p.m. Charges in accordance with state archives regulations

State Library (p. 42), Domplatz 8, Tel. 5 40 14. Monday to Friday from 9 a.m. – 5 p.m., Saturday from 9–12 a.m.; in August, Mon. to Fri. from 9–12 a.m. In addition, 1st Sunday in month for exhibitions

Villa Dessauer – Bamberg Municipal Art Gallery (p. 66), Hainstrasse 4 a, Tel. 87-11 47. Exhibitions change regularly, daily except Monday from 10 a.m. – 4 p.m.

View from the Upper Bridge over the Regnitz to Geyerswörth Castle and the "Lower Mills"

77

Index

Works of art are printed in italics

83